# THE GRIM REAPER

## BY RACHEL LYNETTE

**KIDHAVEN PRESS**
*A part of Gale, Cengage Learning*

GALE
CENGAGE Learning

Detroit • New York • San Francisco • New Haven, Conn • Waterville, Maine • London

## GALE
### CENGAGE Learning™

**LIBRARY OF CONGRESS CATALOGING-IN-PUBLICATION DATA**

Lynette, Rachel.
  The Grim Reaper / by Rachel Lynette.
    p. cm. -- (Monsters)
  Includes bibliographical references and index.
  ISBN 978-0-7377-4568-9 (hardcover)
  1. Grim Reaper (Symbolic character) 2. Monsters--Juvenile literature. I. Title.
  GR75.G65L96 2009
  398'.354--dc22

                                                                          2009025950

KidHaven Press
27500 Drake Rd.
Farmington Hills, MI 48331

ISBN-13: 978-0-7377-4568-9
ISBN-10: 0-7377-4568-1

Printed in the United States of America
1 2 3 4 5 6 7 13 12 11 10 09

Printed by Bang Printing, Brainerd, MN, 1st Ptg., 12/2009

# CONTENTS

# Chapter 1

# Harvester of Souls

An old man lies in a hospital bed. He is pale and thin. He struggles to breathe. The doctor has told his family that the end is near, and they are gathered around his bed. In the corner of the room, invisible to everyone except the dying man, the Grim Reaper waits patiently. He is shrouded in a black robe. His face is covered by a hood. The dying man takes one final, gasping breath, and his body goes still. Now the man stands beside the Grim Reaper, looking at his own lifeless body. Then the Grim Reaper disappears, taking the dead man's soul with him.

# A Skeleton in Dark Robes

The Grim Reaper is a fictional character that **personifies** death. Death is mysterious and frightening to most people. The personified form of death is also mysterious and frightening. In most images, the Grim Reaper is portrayed as a tall, thin figure shrouded in a long, black cloak. His face is usually hidden by a hood. It is clear that under the

*The Grim Reaper is often portrayed as a tall, thin figure shrouded in a long, black cloak. His face is rarely seen and he often carries a scythe.*

cloak, the Grim Reaper is a skeleton because his hands, which are visible, are skinless bones. The Grim Reaper usually carries a **scythe**, and sometimes he also has an hourglass. He rarely speaks. Although this is the most common version of the Grim Reaper, it is not the only one. In some pictures he is simply a skeleton with no robe. In others he is an evil demon; bringing death to everyone he touches.

## THE ANGEL OF DEATH

The Grim Reaper, sometimes called the Angel of Death, or simply Death, has been a part of Western culture for thousands of years. He has appeared in many legends and folktales as well as in art. Although there is no mention of a specific Angel of Death in the *Bible*, there are verses in the Old Testament in which an angel causes death, sometimes many deaths. A verse in the book of *Isaiah* reads, "The angel of the LORD went out and put to death a hundred and eighty-five thousand men in the Assyrian camp. When the people got up the next morning–there were all the dead bodies!"[1] In the New Testament, Death appears in the book of *Revelation*: "I looked and there before me was a pale horse! Its rider was named Death, and Hades was following close behind him. They were given power over a fourth of the earth to kill by sword, famine, and plague and by the wild beasts of the earth."[2]

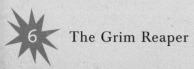

The Grim Reaper is sometimes called the Angel of Death and has appeared in legends, folktales, and art.

The Angel of Death is often confused with Satan. However, in the *Bible*, Satan, though a fallen angel, is never one of the angels who is assigned to kill humans. Satan may get the souls of those who have died, but he does not actually cause death or deliver the souls to hell.

In Islam, the religion of Muslims, the Angel of Death is called Azrael. In some legends, Azrael has four faces and 4,000 wings, and his entire body is made from tongues and eyes—one for each living person on Earth. Azrael spends his time writing and erasing names on a giant scroll. When a person is born, Azrael writes his or her name on the scroll. When a person dies, Azrael erases the name. Azrael himself will be the last to die.

## THE GRIM REAPER IN THE MIDDLE AGES

Death represented as a humanlike figure became popular in the Middle Ages. During this time, the bubonic plague, sometimes called the Black Death, killed over 25 million people, or about a third of Europe's population. Dying of bubonic plague was painful and horrific. In the final stages of the disease, the victim vomits blood. His or her skin turns black, as it is literally **decomposing** while the person is still alive. The body emits a horrible odor. **Seizures** are also common at the time of death.

People were dying everywhere during this horrific period in European history. The artists of the time drew and painted what they saw all around them. The Grim Reaper's skeletal form came from the disease-ravaged, decomposing bodies that were often piled outside the city gates. He is dressed in black because people traditionally wear black after someone has died. Black is also often associ-

*In Norway, during the Middle Ages, the Grim Reaper was personified as an old woman named Pesta who carried a rake and a broom. The rake meant that some people would survive the plague; the broom meant that everyone would die.*

ated with evil and with mystery. His face remains hidden and unknown—just as no one really knows what happens to the souls of the dead.

Although the Grim Reaper is usually portrayed as male, this is not always the case. In Norway death from the plague is personified as an old woman called Pesta, a name which means "plague hag." Pesta could fly, and she traveled throughout the land bringing death wherever she went. She wore a black hood and carried a rake and a broom. If she used the rake, it meant that some people would survive the plague. If she used the broom, all would die.

## REAPING SOULS

The Grim Reaper usually carries a scythe. He uses the scythe to separate the dying person's soul from his or her body. In some pictures from the Middle Ages, the Grim Reaper is seen in a crowd, cutting people down with his scythe as a farmer might cut wheat. However, in most pictures, the Grim Reaper merely stands near the dying person, holding his scythe upright.

In some stories, the Grim Reaper witnesses death, but does not actually cause it. His job is simply to harvest the soul once the person has died. The Grim Reaper then guides the soul to whatever awaits it in the afterlife. In other stories, the Grim Reaper does cause the death, usually by touching the person. In some legends he pours a single drop

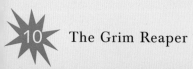

*A wooden engraving by Alfred Rethel portrays Death as a friend. In some stories, the Grim Reaper does not cause death, but guides the soul into the afterlife once the person has died.*

of **gall** into the dying person's mouth to cause death.

## Is the Grim Reaper Evil?

In some pictures and stories the Grim Reaper is portrayed as a demon that enjoys bringing death to humans. However, in most images the Grim Reaper, while frightening and usually unwelcome, is not generally thought to be evil. In most cases, he does not cause death and does not seem to take joy in the death of humans. He is simply doing his job. Death, like birth, is a natural part of life. By doing his job, the Grim Reaper assures that there will be room for new life. In several myths, the Grim Reaper is captured or killed, making it impossible for him to do his job. When this happens, no humans can die and the natural balance of the universe is upset. Eventually, a god or other being releases the Grim Reaper or brings him back to life so that humans can die again and the balance can be restored.

Usually, the Grim Reaper is a silent, solemn figure who shows no emotion. However, in some stories, the Grim Reaper seems to have sympathy for those who are near death. He may grant the person more time, or allow him the chance to win his life with a game. If the death is to be a violent one, he may take the person's soul an instant before death so that the person does not have to endure the physical pain of dying.

# CHAPTER 2

# DEATH AROUND THE WORLD

Cultures all over the world have personified death. Death does not always look like the Western Grim Reaper. Sometimes it is an animal or a monster. Sometimes it is a human man or woman. Many images of death come from religious writings. However, in the West, the Grim Reaper is most frequently found in works of art and in folktales. Often in these tales a human tries to trick the Grim Reaper in order to save himself or herself from death.

## TRICKING DEATH

One story about a human who tries to trick Death

"Godfather Death" is a story written by the Brothers Grimm about a person who tries to trick death.

was written by brothers Jacob and Wilhelm Grimm. In "Godfather Death," a father agrees to make Death his son's godfather. After the boy grows up, Death shows him a special herb in the forest. Death tells the man that he will make him into a famous doctor. Whenever the man sees a patient, Death will appear to him. If Death appears at the patient's head, the doctor can give the patient some of the herb and the patient will recover. If, however, death stands at the patient's feet, the doctor is to say that the patient is beyond help and allow Death to claim him. Then Death warns the doctor not to use the herb without his permission.

The man did indeed become a famous doctor. People all over the land were amazed by how he could tell if a patient would recover or was doomed to die just by looking at him. Then one day the doctor is summoned to the king's bedside. The king is very ill. Death is standing by the king's feet. The doctor decides that just this once he would trick Death, so he picks the king up and turns him around so that his head is now where his feet were. Then he gives the king the herb and the king recovers. However, Death is angry and says to the doctor, "You have betrayed me. I will overlook it this time because you are my godson, but if you dare to do it again, it will cost you your neck, for I will take you yourself away with me."[3]

Not long after the doctor healed the king, the king's only daughter becomes ill. The king proclaims that whoever saves her from death will become her husband and rule the land. When the doctor comes to see the daughter, he is dismayed to see Death standing at the girl's feet. The girl is beautiful, and the doctor wants to be king and so he repeats his trick. He turns the girl around and gives her the herb. The girl recovers, and Death is angry. He tells the doctor, "You are finished. Now it is your turn."[4] Death grabs the doctor and takes him to an underground cavern. In the cavern the doctor sees thousands of burning candles. Some are large while others are nearly burnt out. Death tells the doctor that each candle represents a human life. The doctor asks to see his candle, which he thought would be large. He is shocked to see that it is barely a stump and that the flame is sputtering. The doctor begs for a new candle, but rather than grant his wish, Death puts his candle out and the doctor immediately falls to the ground, dead.

In most European folktales about tricking Death, a human may succeed once or twice, but in the end, Death takes his revenge. The same holds true in Greek myths about Thanatos, the god of death.

## DEATH IN GREEK MYTHOLOGY

Thanatos is the Greek god of peaceful death. Thanatos comes from a rather gloomy family. His parents are the gods of night and darkness, and his twin brother is Hypnos, the god of sleep. Other siblings include the gods of doom, envy, suffering,

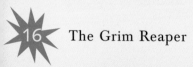

The Grim Reaper

*In Greek mythology, Sisyphos was not able to trick death and his punishment for trying was to roll a boulder up a hill for all eternity.*

and blame. His bloodthirsty sisters, the Keres, are the spirits of violent death.

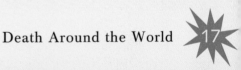

Yama. Yama has green skin, wears red clothes, and rides a black buffalo. In one hand, Yama carries a **mace**, which he uses to strike down his victims. In the other hand he carries a noose, which he uses to drag his victims to his dark

and gloomy palace. At his palace, Yama sits on his throne and judges the soul of the now-dead person. His assistant, Chitagupta, keeps detailed records of each person's life, recording his or her good and evil deeds in the *Book of Destiny*. If Yama judges that the person has lived a good life, the person goes to heaven. If he or she has lived a bad life, the person goes to one of several hells. If the person's life was not particularly good or bad, he or she is sent back to Earth to try again.

*Yama is the Hindu god of death. He decides if a person goes to heaven, one of several hells, or back to Earth to try life again*

Yama is feared by mortals, most of whom are not ready to die when he comes for them. This was the case with Markandeya. The god Shiva gave Markandeya's parents a choice before he was born. They could have a foolish son who would live 100 years or a wise one who would live for just sixteen years. The parents choose to have a wise son. Markandeya was not only wise but also devoted to Shiva.

On the day of his sixteenth birthday, Markandeya was worshipping Shiva by praying to an idol of Shiva. When the boy saw Yama coming for him, he clung to the idol and prayed for protection. Yama tried to capture Markandeya with his noose, but when he threw it, the rope encircled the idol of Shiva along with Markandeya. This made Shiva angry. Shiva burst out of the idol and kicked Yama to death. With Yama dead, no mortals could die. The other gods knew this would throw the universe off balance, so they begged Shiva to bring Yama back to life. Shiva agreed, but only in exchange for Markandeya's life. Rather than dying on his sixteenth birthday, Markandeya ended up living forever as a sixteen-year-old.

Markandeya escaped Death. No one escaped Death in ancient Egypt, however. Egyptians who were deemed worthy were **embalmed** by the god Anubis and went on to live in the afterlife. Those who were not worthy lost their lives forever.

# Guardian of the Egyptian Dead

Anubis is an ancient god. He has the body of a man and the head of a jackal. His head is black because an embalmed body turns black. Anubis, whose job is to watch over the embalming process, invented embalming and mummification, a process which preserves a dead body and keeps it from decaying. According to Egyptian myths, Anubis is the son of the goddess Nephthys. However, Nephthys abandoned him in the wilderness when he was a baby. He was found by the goddess Isis who, along with her husband, Osiris, raised Anubis. When Anubis was grown, Osiris's brother, Set, murdered Osiris and **dismembered** his body. Isis found all of the pieces and brought them to Anubis. Anubis embalmed and mummified his foster father so that he could live again and rule the underworld.

It is also Anubis's job to lead the dead to the underworld. Once there, he balances the newly dead person's heart on a scale against the Feather of Truth. If the person had lived a good and honest life, his or her heart would be lighter than the feather, and the soul was permitted to journey on into the afterlife. If the person had been evil and dishonest, and his or her heart was heavier than the feather, it was immediately eaten by the demon Ammit. Ammit had the head of a crocodile, the body of a leopard, and the hindquarters of a hippopotamus. If a person's heart was eaten by Ammit,

*Anubis, who has the body of a man and the head of a jackal, is an ancient god who leads the dead to the underworld. He uses a scale to balance a dead person's heart against the Feather of Truth.*

then his or her soul was destroyed and the person was dead forever.

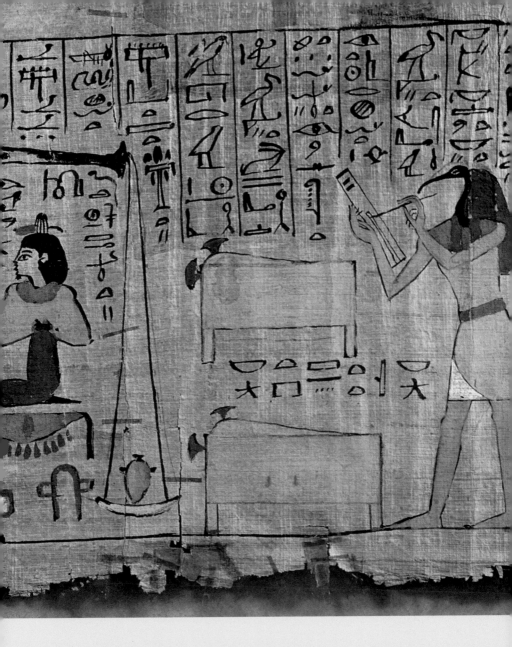

## THE BALANCE OF LIFE AND DEATH IN AFRICA

In the folktale "Life and Death," the Hausa tribe of Western Africa view death not as frightening or judgmental, but rather as a part of the circle of life. In the story, Life and Death are represented as two old men who are traveling together. One day they come to a spring and ask the owner for permission to drink. The owner of the spring grants permission, saying that the older of the two must drink first, as is the custom. Life and Death each claim to be older than the other. Life argues that he must be older because without living things, Death cannot exist. Death claims that before there was Life, everything was Death and that Life comes from Death and then returns to it again. Therefore Death must be older. Finally, they ask the owner of the spring to settle the argument. The owner says,

> How can one speak of Death without Life, from which it proceeds? And how can one speak of Life without Death, to which all living things go? Both of you have spoken eloquently. Your words are true. Neither of you is senior. Neither of you is junior. Life and Death are merely two faces of the Creator. Therefore you are of equal age. Here is a gourd of water. Drink from it together.[5]

 The Grim Reaper

# CHAPTER 3

# DEATH IN POP CULTURE

The poem "Because I Could Not Stop for Death" by American poet Emily Dickinson was first published in 1890. In it Death is portrayed as a kind gentleman, perhaps even a **suitor**. Portraying Death as kind and gentle, even welcome, is a big change from the frightening Death of the Middle Ages. In addition to poems, personified death can be found in books, movies, TV shows, and even video games. Sometimes the Grim Reaper is silent and frightening, much like the Grim Reaper in the Middle Ages. However, sometimes modern writers take a lighter approach. Today the character of Death might be friendly, clumsy, or silly. Perhaps when people can laugh at Death, it makes death less frightening.

## A New Take on Death

Author Terry Pratchett does not take Death too seriously in his series of books about another world, called Discworld. Although Pratchett's Death looks like the traditional Grim Reaper, he is not all that scary. He is fascinated by humans and often tries to imitate their behaviors. This is why he lives in a house, even though he has no need of a kitchen, bedroom, or bathroom since he does not need to eat, sleep, or use the bathroom.

Death also rides a white horse called Binky. Before choosing Binky, Death tried a skeletal horse, but pieces kept falling off and he had to keep stopping to wire them back on. He also tried a fiery steed, but it caught his barn and his robe on fire, so in the end, he settled for a real horse.

One of Death's companions is the Death of Rats, sometimes called the Grim Squeaker. The Grim Squeaker is a skeletal rat who stands on his hind legs, wears a black robe, and carries a tiny scythe. His job is to harvest the souls of rodents.

In one of Pratchett's books, Hogfather, who is like Santa Claus in Discworld, disappears. Death decides to take his place, complete with a fake beard and a red coat. Although Death tries to do the right thing, he makes some mistakes. For example, he often gives children exactly what they

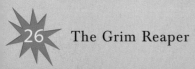

*Terry Pratchett (pictured) takes a lighter approach to the character of Death in his Discworld series.*

ask for. In one case, this meant a real sword for a six-year-old and a pony for a girl who lives on the third floor of an apartment building. While Pratchett takes a light approach to Death in his books, the author of the Harry Potter books takes death much more seriously.

## DEATHLY DEMENTORS

The popular Harry Potter books by J.K. Rowling are full of witches, trolls, dragons, and other magical creatures. Although there is no single character representing death, Rowling did create the dementors. The dementors look similar to the Grim Reaper. They are tall and thin. They wear long robes and seem to be made of decomposing flesh. Rather than walking, dementors glide. In the book, *Harry Potter and the Prisoner of Azkaban*, a teacher explains the dementors to Harry:

> Dementors are among the foulest creatures that walk this earth. They infest the darkest, filthiest places, they glory in decay and despair, they drain peace, hope and happiness out of the air around them. Even Muggles [nonmagical people] feel their presence, though they can't see them. Get too near a Dementor and every good feeling, every happy memory, will be sucked out of you. If it can, the Dementor will feed on you long enough to reduce you to something like

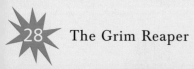

*In her Harry Potter series, J.K. Rowling created the dementors, who look similar to Death. In* Harry Potter and the Prisoner of Azkaban, *the dementors guard Azkaban prison and feast on the happy memories of its prisoners.*

itself–soulless and evil. You'll be left with nothing but the worst experiences of your life.[6]

Dementors are used to guard Azkaban, a prison for witches and wizards who have committed crimes. There they feast on the happy memories of the prisoners, most of whom go insane within a few weeks. Whenever Harry encounters a dementor, he is forced to relive the worst moment of his life: his parents' murder. In addition to forcing a person to relive his worst memories, a dementor can also suck out a person's soul. This is called the Dementor's Kiss. A person who has had the soul sucked out of him continues to live, but only as a shell–the person's mind is gone, never to return. This is considered to be a fate worse than death.

## Death in the Comics

Images of the Grim Reaper have appeared in several comic books, including *Superman* and *The Incredible Hulk.* However, in *Sandman,* written by Neil Gaiman and illustrated by Mike Dringenberg, Death looks very different than the traditional skeleton in robes.

*Sandman* was published by DC Comics from 1988 to 1996 and was 75 issues long. In these comic books, death is portrayed as an attractive **goth** woman in her early twenties. Her skin is pale, and she dresses all in black–usually black jeans and

*Neil Gaiman poses with new* Sandman *illustrations in New York in 1999. The Grim Reaper has appeared in comic books like the* Sandman *series, written by Gaiman and illustrated by Mike Dringenberg, looking very different from Death's traditional portrayal.*

a black top. She also wears a large silver **ankh** around her neck. Despite her grim job, Death is generally cheerful and pleasant.

According to the *Sandman* comic books, Death appears to every human twice during his or her lifetime. The first time is at birth, when she talks to the newborn. The second time is at death, when she escorts the person to the afterlife. Once each century, Death must take the form of a human who will die that day. By feeling what it is like to be human and to die, Death gains an understanding of the value of the lives she takes.

In *Sandman*, Death is often the nurturing older sister of the main character, Dream. Although she does not appear very often in the series, she is one of its most popular characters. *Empire* magazine names *Sandman's* Death the fifteenth greatest comic book character on its list of 50, saying, "Perhaps it's because Death's duties make such cheerfulness double-edged, and because she has an air of mystery about her that gives her incalculable depth. What's more, she's the wise elder sister that everyone wishes they had."[7]

## ANIMATED DEATH

The Grim Reaper has appeared on several TV shows including *Animaniacs* and *The Simpsons*. In *The Simpsons*, the Grim Reaper appears in the 2003 Halloween episode, "Tree House of Horror XIV," when he comes for Homer's son, Bart. After a humorous chase scene, Homer saves his son by killing the Grim Reaper with a bowling ball. Of course with the Grim Reaper dead, no one can die. Homer is

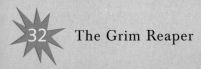

not happy about this and mourns the Grim Reaper saying, "Death, Death, we miss you so much! You were the busboy in the restaurant of life . . . and you made Nascar racing exciting."[8] When Homer tries on the dead Grim Reaper's robe, he becomes Death himself. This does not work out very well and eventually God decides to let Homer return to his life.

## DEATH IS A GIRL NAMED GEORGE

In the Showtime TV series *Dead Like Me*, which aired from 2003 to 2005, there are several Grim Reapers and one of them is the main character of the series. In the first episode, a depressed young woman named George (short for Georgia) is killed when a toilet seat falls to Earth from the Mir space station. However, instead of moving on to the afterlife, George must serve as a Grim Reaper.

Along with a group of other reapers, George must harvest the souls of people who die in accidents or from murders or suicides, ideally, just before they die. This can be challenging as she is often given sketchy information about the time and place the death is to take place. If she fails to harvest the soul, it will be trapped inside the dead body.

## THE GRIM REAPER IN THE MOVIES

The Grim Reaper has also appeared in several movies. Perhaps one of the most famous is the Swedish film, *The Seventh Seal*. The film was made in 1957 and takes place in the Middle Ages. In the

The Grim Reaper has appeared in several movies, including Ingmar Bergman's The Seventh Seal, which was produced in 1957.

film, Death is a pale man in a hooded cloak. At the start of the film, a knight returns to his homeland after ten years at war only to find people dying of the black plague. When Death comes for him, he challenges Death to a game of chess for his life. During the game, the knight questions the meaning of life. In the end, he loses the game of chess, but is able to trick Death in order to save a young family. By saving the family, the knight finds that there was indeed meaning to his life.

In the 1934 movie *Death Takes a Holiday*, Death takes human form to find out why people are always afraid of him. While he is human, a young woman falls in love with him. Although he loves her, too, he first tries to scare her away by allowing her to see his true form. It turns out that she has always seen him this way, and so he allows her to come with him when he returns to his job harvesting souls.

In 1998 *Death Takes a Holiday* was remade as *Meet Joe Black.* In this remake, actor Brad Pitt plays the part of Death. In this movie Death borrows the body of a young man who just died in an auto accident. He enjoys his time as a human, taking delight in simple things, like the taste of peanut butter. Eventually he falls in love with a young woman but soon realizes that the woman does not love him, but rather the man whose body he has borrowed. In the end, he brings the young man back to life and then goes back to his job.

The Grim Reaper

# THE GRIM REAPER IN VIDEO GAMES

In addition to TV and movies, the Grim Reaper has appeared as a character in several video games. In Guitar Hero, players compete by having their character play songs. The player must hit notes accurately to win points. An audience reacts with cheers or boos depending on how well the player is doing. One of the characters is a skeletal, horned character called the Grim Ripper, who plays a scythe with guitar strings. At the start of the game, the character is hidden. Players use game currency to unlock the Reaper to use as a playable character. Grim Ripper is described as "tearing it up from the

*The Grim Reaper has also appeared in video games, such as Guitar Hero (shown here on the Nintendo Wii). In this game, he is called the Grim Ripper, who plays a scythe with guitar strings.*

beyond, Grim is a full-on rocker. Grim has abandoned the stealing of souls for the rush of stealing the show and now tours the world laying down monster riffs."[9] In Castlevania, the Grim Reaper teams with Dracula to try to defeat the player. He usually attacks with sickles that he pulls from the air. In The Sims, a game in which players create characters that simulate real life, the Grim Reaper appears when a character is about to die. The player can opt to play a game to save the character's life. If the player wins, the character lives on. If not, the Grim Reaper collects the character and he or she is gone from the game forever.

Because the Grim Reaper is a personification of death created by humans, his image will most likely continue to change, at least a little, with each new author or artist. Sometimes frightening and mysterious, sometimes comical or even sympathetic, images of death help people to cope with the reality that everyone dies eventually. In the words of Death himself from the film *The Seventh Seal*: "Nothing escapes me. No *one* escapes me."[10]

# NOTES

## CHAPTER 1: HARVESTER OF SOULS

1. *Isaiah* 37:36 (New International Version).
2. *Revelation* 6:8 (New International Version).

## CHAPTER 2: DEATH AROUND THE WORLD

3. Jacob Grimm and Wilhelm Grimm, "Godfather Death," www.pitt.edu/~dash/grimm044 .html.
4. Grimm and Grimm, "Godfather Death."
5. Jarold Courlander, *A Treasury of African Folklore*, New York: Marlowe, 1996, p. 57.

## CHAPTER 3: DEATH IN POP CULTURE

6. J.K. Rowling, *Harry Potter and the Prisoner of Azkaban*, New York: Scholastic, 2004, p. 203.
7. *Empire*, "The 50 Greatest Comic Book Characters," *Empire*, www.empireonline .com/50greatestcomiccharacters/default .asp?c=15.
8. "Tree House of Horror XIV." DVD. Directed by Steven Dean Moore, Twentieth Century Fox Television, Hollywood, CA. Original air date: November 2, 2003.

9. Guitar Hero, video game, developed by Harmonix, Sunnyvale, CA: RedOctane, 2005.

10. *The Seventh Seal (Det Sjunde Inseglet)*, directed by Ingmar Bergman, Stockholm, Sweden: Svensk Filmindustri, 1958 (USA), The Internet Movie Database, www.imdb.com/title/tt0050976/quotes.

# Glossary

**ankh:** A symbol of life from ancient Egypt.

**decomposing:** Rotting or decaying.

**dismembered:** To take the limbs off of a human body.

**embalmed:** Using chemicals to keep a dead body from decaying.

**gall:** A bitter liquid.

**goth:** A style consisting of black clothing, black eye makeup and lipstick, and heavy, silver jewelry.

**mace:** A heavy club with a round, spiked top.

**mortal:** A human who will eventually die.

**personifies:** An animal, object, or idea with human traits.

**scythe:** A tool with a long pole and a curved blade.

**seizures:** A sudden attack of an illness that causes uncontrollable body movements.

**shackles:** Metal rings connected with a chain fastened around a person's wrists or ankles.

**suitor:** A man who courts a woman in order to get her to marry him.

41

# FOR FURTHER EXPLORATION

## BOOKS

Joshua Gee, *Encyclopedia Horrifica: The Terrifying TRUTH! About Vampires, Ghosts, Monsters, and More.* New York: Scholastic, 2007. This interesting and informative book tells about all kinds of monsters, including the Grim Reaper.

Roger Lancelyn Green, *Tales of Ancient Egypt.* New York: Puffin, 1996. This book features stories from ancient Egypt. The Egyptian god of death, Anubis, is included in some of the stories.

Jacob Grimm and Wilhelm Grimm, *The Juniper Tree and Other Tales from Grimm.* New York: Farrar, Straus and Giroux, 2003. This is a collection of 27 of the Grimms' darkest tales, including "Godfather Death." The book is illustrated by Maurice Sendak, the author and illustrator of the award-winning book, *Where the Wild Things Are.*

Anthony Horowitz, *Myths and Legends.* Boston: Kingfisher, 2007. This volume of myths from around the world includes a story about Yama, the Hindu god of death, and a tale from Western Africa about a boy who meets Death.

J.K. Rowling, *Harry Potter and the Prisoner of Azka-*

*ban.* New York: Scholastic, 2004. In this book, the third in the Harry Potter series, Harry meets the dementors and learns how to defeat them.

Tere Stouffer, *The Complete Idiot's Guide to the World of Harry Potter.* New York: Alpha Books, 2007. This book includes information about dementors.

Diane Zahler, *The Black Death.* Minneapolis: Twenty-First Century Books, 2009. This book describes how the Black Death affected Europe during the Middle Ages. It includes a time line, a glossary, a who's who, and a list of suggested titles and Web sites for further reading.

## INTERNET SOURCES

Brothers Grimm, "Godfather Death," All Family Resources, www.familymanagement.com/literacy/grimms/grimms33.html.

Indian Divinity, "Yama," Indian Divinity, www.webonautics.com/mythology/yama.html.

Caroline Seawright, "Anubis, God of Embalming and Guide and Friend of the Dead," Kunoichi's Home Page, October 8, 2001, www.thekeep.org/~kunoichi/kunoichi/themestream/anubis.html.

## WEB SITES

**TheMiddleAges.net** (www.themiddleages.net). This Web site provides information about the Middle Ages, including a section on the bubonic plague.

**WatchTheSimpsonsOnline** (www.wtso.net). On this Web site, viewers can watch episodes of the TV program *The Simpsons*, including the episode, "Tree House of Horror XIV," from season fifteen. In this episode Homer Simpson kills Death.

# INDEX

The Grim Reaper

# PICTURE CREDITS

# ABOUT THE AUTHOR

Rachel Lynette is happy to report that she is still alive and has not yet met the Grim Reaper. Lynette has written over 40 books for children of all ages as well as resource materials for teachers. She lives in the Seattle, Washington, area with her two delightful children, David and Lucy, and a cat named Cosette. When she is not writing, Lynette enjoys spending time with her family and friends, traveling, reading, drawing, crocheting colorful hats, biking, and in-line skating.